TRUTH
Laced with
Grace

CHARIS ROOKS

Truth Laced with Grace: 31 Purpose Driven Devotions for Women
Copyright 2017 by Charis Rooks

Published by Inspired Grace Media Productions
www.igmproductions.com
Cover Design and Typesetting by Dark Wish Designs

All Rights Reserved. This book, or parts thereof may not be reproduced in any form, stored in a retrieval system, or transmitted in any form by any means - electronic, mechanical, photocopy, recording, or otherwise - without prior written permission of the publisher, except as provided by The United States of America Copyright Law.

All Scripture quotations are taken from the Holy Bible, New International Version. Copyright 1973, 1978, 1984, 2011 by Biblica, Inc. The "NIV" and "New International Version" are trademarks registered in the United States Patent and Trademark Office by Biblica, Inc.

While the author has made every effort to provide accurate addresses for the internet at the time of publication, neither the publisher nor the author assumes any responsibility for errors or changes that occur after publication.

Printed in the United States of America

Dedication

This book is dedicated to women like myself who feel unqualified at times and for women who heard God call them to a place, but have fears that they will disappoint God upon arrival. This book is for women that doubt their purpose when doubt has no place in their lives, or in their ultimate purpose.

Esther 4:14

"For if you remain silent at this time, relief and deliverance for the Jews will arise from another place, but you and your father's family will perish. And who knows but that you have come to your royal position for such a time as this?"

Contents

Dedication 3
Contents 4
Introduction 6
My Prayer for You 11
Unqualified Women in the Bible 12
Day 1 13
Day 2 15
Day 3 21
Day 4 25
Day 5 29
Day 6 31
Day 7 37
Day 8 41
Day 9 45
Day 10 49
Day 11 53
Day 12 57
Day 13 61
Day 14 63
Day 15 69
Day 16 73
Day 17 75
Day 18 81

Day 19	85
Day 20	89
Day 21	93
Day 22	97
Day 23	101
Day 24	105
Day 25	109
Day 26	113
Day 27	117
Day 28	121
Day 29	125
Day 30	129
Day 31	133
About the Author	137
Contact Information	145

Introduction

When I was a teenager, I was not what you would consider "the average teenager." I had a desire to go into ministry, but I was afraid in the same breath. It was something that I loved, but also something that no one around me talked about doing. As a teen, stepping out of the norm was very difficult. Everyone around me wanted to be a lawyer, a doctor, a pop star, or an athlete. Contrary to this, I decided early for me it would be ministry. I remember one youth group trip, I found myself on stage standing behind a microphone, sharing the love that I had for Christ. That day, I felt at home, sharing my testimony in front of a couple hundred students. I was so excited I rushed home to tell everyone this was my calling, that I have a purpose, and I knew my assignment. I had decided I was going into ministry.

As you may guess, not everyone was receptive to the news. Close friends, and even some family members, told me that I had no business going into ministry. I wasn't qualified, or I was too young to teach anyone about Jesus, and those were the nicer versions of their opinionated comments. So, I struggled for years not stepping up and operating in the assignment God had given me because of the doubt that I had accepted from others, for myself. The negative seed was planted, and I spent most of my young adult life nurturing it. As I nurtured my doubt, it grew daily, and I walked further and further away from my calling. As I grew older, circumstances in my life led me to believe that ministry was not for me, and by the time I went through my second divorce, it seemed as if all hope for the ministry was wiped away. I had begun to allow myself to believe what others said to my face: "No one will listen to you," "You are damaged goods," "You reflect what many women fear and do not want in their relationships," and "Women will not listen to you; they will more than likely laugh at you."

So, I began to think, "How in the world can I offer anything to anyone, especially women?" Thank God, I learned shortly after that, my two divorces were not my qualifier, God is. It's funny now;

I have realized over the years that I do my best work and my most rewarding work as an unqualified woman by society's standard, just in sharing my testimony. But then of course shortly after I felt a little bit of confidence, doubt returned. I started to feel that even though God qualified me, and my testimony seemed to assist others, it still wasn't enough because of the fear I had and rejection I was subject to. When I was younger, I would think to myself how hard it must be, not knowing what I should be doing. Now as an adult I must say, knowing that I was called to ministry and dragging my feet hurt more than any pain I have ever encountered. My spiritual life suffered for many years because I knew I had an assignment, but I wasn't operating in it because of fear and the possibility of rejection.

I also battled with not stepping into that role, in fear that I would disappoint God and hurt his people more than help them. I questioned God many times, asking, "Why me? I'm no one special. For goodness sake, I have divorced twice making me a severely broken woman. I am sure God; you do not want to use me." I battled myself mentally daily, waging in spiritual warfare against myself and never letting go to let God fight for me. So, amidst the warfare while waiting for my answer from God, I decided to go back to school. I earned my bachelor's degree, became certified in Divorce Coaching, started my MBA with a concentration in Leadership, and made sure I was well prepared just in case God was in fact going to use me. You will never guess what happened after I graduated with my MBA in Leadership. I started to tell myself that I still was not qualified. I couldn't believe it. I still felt unqualified. Then, the day finally came when I realized that I could not live like this anymore. I knew I was wasting time, and somewhere out there was a woman depending on me to share my testimony. Enough was enough and no amount of degrees or certifications will make me feel ready. My degrees did not define my purpose; they are simply tools to assist me with my assignments.

I also realized God can use me without a degree. There is no law stating that I cannot operate in my purpose without a degree or certification. So, I began to pray a simple prayer, "Use me, God, even though I feel useless and I have no clue how you will use me for your will." Since praying that prayer, I have seen myself in a different light. I see a reflection of confidence, hope, purpose, and determination. Also, because of this prayer I now recognize the lies the enemy tried to convince me was truth to draw me further away from my assignment. However, now I'm excited to say I know the "Truth" and so can you because it is "Laced with God's Grace."

My Prayer for You

I thank God today for my sister in Christ who is reading this book and her journey towards understanding the purpose you have destined for her. God, I thank you for showing her that a title is not the only qualification for being called. Thank you, God, for showing her that once she is called to her assignment in life, there is work that must be done, dedication to doing it, and purpose no matter the title that she may or may not hold. Thank you for letting her know, God, that answering your call to her personal assignment only requires that she have the willingness to say "yes" to you and to show up ready for your guidance and instruction. I thank you God for your love and unmerited favor in my sister's life.

In Jesus' Name, I Pray,

Amen

Charis R.

Unqualified Women in the Bible

The Samaritan woman was a multiple divorcee, Miriam was a gossiper, Martha was a worrier, Sara was impatient, Naomi was an old widow, Esther was orphan child, and Rehab was a prostitute. God doesn't call the qualified; God qualifies the called!

Day 1

Affirmation

I Have Been Called

Devotion

When you are called, you are called; no one can change what God has called you to do. Even if someone tries to manipulate it so that you fail, God will reverse it so that you succeed. Understand that your calling is YOUR CALLING. No one can steal that from you, and no one can move into your calling no matter what qualifications they may have. Go forward today, and know that you are qualified by God, and no one can stop what God has chosen you to do.

Encouragement Scripture

John 15:16

"You didn't choose me. I chose you. I appointed you to go and produce lasting fruit, so that the Father will give you whatever you ask for, using my name.

TRUTH LACED WITH GRACE

CHARIS ROOKS

Day 2

Affirmation
I Am Enough

Devotion

Understand that you are your biggest challenge. When it comes to not feeling qualified, you are the main power holding you back from doing the work that God has assigned you to do. God is the only one that knows the right path for you. Go forward today, and know that whatever your path is, God has already created your map - you just need to follow it. He will be with you every step of the way. God made you exactly as he intended. Even when you feel that you are not enough, God made you this way for a reason, and God makes no mistakes.

Encouragement Scripture

Proverbs 3:6

"Seek HIS will in all you do, and he will show you which path to take."

CHARIS ROOKS

Day 3

Affirmation

I Have A Purpose

Devotion

Some think it must be difficult not knowing what their purpose is, and not knowing what they should be doing. However, knowing your purpose and dragging your feet hurts more than any pain you will ever encounter. This is because your spirit hurts. It knows you need help, not only to become a more effective leader, but to be a fearless spiritual warrior for Christ through testimony. Go forward today, and know that God has given you a purpose that is unique to you and you alone.

Encouragement Scripture

Exodus 9:16

"But, I have spared you for a purpose - to show you my power, and to spread my fame throughout the earth."

TRUTH LACED WITH GRACE

CHARIS ROOKS

Day 4

Affirmation

I Will Make a New Friend Today Not Only

Will They Be Blessed, But So Will I

Devotion

Have you walked around and felt out of place, and then, suddenly, a scenario plays out right before you: Someone is strategically placed in front of you, and you hear them speaking, and know this is your opportunity to share your testimony? That is the point in which God gives us opportunities, and many of us start to analyze to the point that fear, or distraction sets in. Sharing your testimony is a part of your healing, and when you refuse to share, you refuse to allow God to completely heal you. Stop running, and start looking forward to the moments that God has orchestrated to release healing over your life through your testimony. Don't analyze. Don't talk yourself out of it - just take the opportunity and share your testimony. Even when you feel uneasy, God has it all planned out and has allowed this moment to come to pass.

Encouragement Scripture

Psalm 66:16

"Come and listen, all you who fear God, and I will tell you what he did for me."

TRUTH LACED WITH GRACE

CHARIS ROOKS

Day 5

Affirmation

God Is with Me

Devotion

God says, "I will never leave you nor forsake you." There will be days that you feel so unequipped and alone. This is when you must know and believe that God is with you. Do not get caught up in all the distractions of the world, for it is only when you tune out the distraction and turn up the voice of God that you will discover God is equipping you with everything you will need. He knows your assignment and knows what you need to complete this assignment that He has given to you.

Encouragement Scripture

Deuteronomy 31:8

"Do not be afraid or discouraged, for the Lord will personally go ahead of you. He will be with you; he will neither fail you nor abandon you."

TRUTH LACED WITH GRACE

CHARIS ROOKS

Day 6

Affirmation

I Am Loved

Devotion

God loves you so much that He has created pit stops along the way called, "divine appointments." These appointments are there to show you that you are on the right path. They will direct you when you feel lost, and satisfy you when you feel unequipped. They bring enlightenment, hope, and healing to you at the most unplanned moments of your life. Whenever you have a divine appointment, stop and pray a prayer of thanks and gratitude. Communicate with God, and know that God loves you. God will never forsake you, HIS love is eternal, and GOD will continue to love you if you allow him to.

Encouragement Scripture

John 3:16

"For this is how God loved the world: He gave his one and only Son, so that everyone who believes in Him will not perish, but have eternal life."

TRUTH LACED WITH GRACE

CHARIS ROOKS

Day 7

Affirmation

I Will Let My Faith Be Bigger Than My Fear

Devotion

Do not condition yourself to believe the lies that the enemy has told you. Instead condition yourself to respond only to the voice of GOD. How do you do this? You must first know God and communicate with God. You will do both through daily reading of your bible and prayer. Do not get caught up on the length of prayer or the technicality of prayer because the enemy will lie to you and make you believe that your prayers are not good or formal enough for God. Your prayers are just that, YOUR prayers. Talk to God authentically, no matter how you are feeling. Don't forget to thank God daily for your calling, purpose, His love, grace, and mercy.

Encouragement Scripture

2 Timothy 1:7

"For God has not given us a spirit of fear and timidity, but of power, love, and self-discipline."

TRUTH LACED WITH GRACE

CHARIS ROOKS

Day 8

Affirmation

I Am Strong

Devotion

In the early stages of your calling, it is not uncommon for you to not be able to sleep. This is especially true if you are trying to run from your calling in hope that it is given to someone else, or if you have come to the point in which you have trained yourself to believe that you have misunderstood what God has said. Know that God will not outsource your calling for you. This means that God will not go through several other people to test your calling on them. Your calling is just that, YOUR CALLING! You were created for such a time as this. When all seems too difficult to handle, turn to God for comfort for he will help you accomplish your goal.

Encouragement Scripture

Esther 4:14

"If you keep quiet at a time like this, deliverance and relief for the Jews will arise from some other place, but you and your relatives will die. Who knows if perhaps you were made queen for just such a time as this?"

TRUTH LACED WITH GRACE

CHARIS ROOKS

TRUTH LACED WITH GRACE

Affirmation

I Will Celebrate Myself Because I am A Divine Original

Devotion

You are a unique original. What does that mean? God created you, not as a copy or an imitation, but you have been created purposefully from the top of your head, to the bottom of your feet. Along with this is your calling which has also been created purposely and uniquely original. Therefore, it is not by mistake or coincidence that your specific calling has been assigned to you. Knowing that you and your calling are unique originals, move forward, and make it a point to wake up every day and say, "God use me for your will and not my own."

Encouragement Scripture

Psalm 139:13-14

"You made all the delicate, inner parts of my body and knit me together in my mother's womb. Thank you for making me so wonderfully complex! Your workmanship is marvelous - how well I know it."

TRUTH LACED WITH GRACE

CHARIS ROOKS

Day 10

Affirmation

I Will Stand Tall in My Calling

Devotion

There will be times where you feel so unworthy, unqualified, and not the best choice by any means. Remember that your calling requires you to let go of your idea of worthiness, qualifications, and "best choice" determination. If you stay stuck in that mindset, you block God from moving you through the process of preparation. While you are busy worrying about being qualified, God is working, creating in you the needed components to make you qualified by HIS standards, not your own. Move forward when you feel these thoughts creeping in and say out loud, "I am worthy, I am qualified, and I am the best choice."

Encouragement Scripture

1 Corinthians 6:11

"Some of you were once like that. But you were cleansed; you were made holy; you were made right with God by calling on the name of the Lord Jesus Christ and by the Spirit of our God."

TRUTH LACED WITH GRACE

CHARIS ROOKS

TRUTH LACED WITH GRACE

Affirmation

God Is Bigger Than All My Fear

Devotion

There may be times that you fear what others will think of or say about you. Do you know that God sent His son, Jesus Christ, who died for our sins on the cross?

As you fear what others are saying, think about how Jesus felt as he carried the cross through the city. You will be mocked, laughed at, and teased, but that will not deter God from helping you to accomplish your purpose. Accept that and move forward, knowing that no matter what is said; you have a relationship with God. God is your source, not those who mock you and stab you in the back. Pray for those who mistreat you and speak negativity in your life, and then move on. Your call requires you to spend time focusing on God and not on the feedback of man. As you spend time with

God, He will strengthen and uphold you.

Encouragement Scripture

Isaiah 41:10

"Don't be afraid, for I am with you. Don't be discouraged, for I am your God. I will strengthen you and help you. I will hold you up with my victorious right hand."

TRUTH LACED WITH GRACE

CHARIS ROOKS

Day 12

Affirmation

I Will Never Give Up

Devotion

There are several strategies that the enemy uses to keep you from progressing forward in your calling, and one of those strategies is to attack your self-esteem. If your self-esteem is low, then you will start to doubt what God says about you. If you allow that same doubt to creep in, it will take over and hold your faith hostage. You will then start to struggle when it comes to completing the tasks God has called you to. You must never give up because God created you uniquely, just as he created everyone else with their own uniqueness to fulfill a calling.

Encouragement Scripture

Philippians 4:13

"For I can do everything through Christ, who gives me strength."

TRUTH LACED WITH GRACE

CHARIS ROOKS

Day 13

Affirmation

The World Needs Leaders and I Am One

Devotion

The world is full of followers - people that are content to sit by and watch as others take the lead and make a real difference. The world does not need any more followers. The world needs leaders, and God has given you the strength, the fortitude, and the testimony to step into the leadership role that he has created for you. Take the chance; step out and lead those around you in the ways of God and in the ways of true belief. You are so much stronger than you believe. God has seen that and has prepared a tailor-made path and calling that will reflect your strengths and help you to fulfill your destiny. The world needs leaders, and, believe it or not, you were destined to be one of them.

Encouragement Scripture

Mark 10:45 New Living Translation (NLT)

"For even the Son of Man came not to be served but to serve others and to give his life as a ransom for many."

TRUTH LACED WITH GRACE

CHARIS ROOKS

TRUTH LACED WITH GRACE

Affirmation

I Will Not Worry About Everyday Life

Devotion

Your everyday life is certain to weigh heavy on your heart. You must go to the grocery store, clean the house, and care for the family… but you are worth so much more than you can ever know. There are women that feel that their everyday lives prevent them from doing something great, and that it keeps them from fulfilling their true purpose. This is simply not the case. God will work in you to make you strong enough to see that you are more than your everyday life and that you are more than your struggles.

Encouragement Scripture

Matthew 6:25-27 New Living Translation (NLT)

"That is why I tell you not to worry about everyday life -whether you have enough food and drink, or enough clothes to wear. Isn't life more than food and your body more than clothing? Look at the birds. They don't plant, or harvest, or store food in barns, for your heavenly Father feeds them. And aren't you far more valuable to him than they are? Can all your worries add a single moment to your life?

TRUTH LACED WITH GRACE

CHARIS ROOKS

#

Affirmation

God Is Always with Me Because Jesus Died for Me

Devotion

God sent His only son to die on the cross not only to atone for the sins of man, but to also give birth to a closer relationship with His followers and His children. Because Jesus died, we now can be closer to God than ever before. We have the chance to be one with God, and to have the true delight and opportunity to have God in our everyday lives, helping us to work through any struggle we might be feeling.

Encouragement Scripture

Romans 5:10

"For since our friendship with God was restored by the death of His Son while we were still His enemies, we will certainly be saved through the life of His Son."

TRUTH LACED WITH GRACE

CHARIS ROOKS

Day 16

Affirmation

My Accomplishments Bring Great Joy to God

Devotion

Every wonderful thing you do, everything that you accomplish not only brings joy to you and your family, it also brings glory and joy to God. He created you to do so many wonderful things, and each time that you are successful, each time you accomplish a goal, or fulfill a purpose, He looks down from Heaven and beams at your strength and accomplishment. Each great thing we do can be reflected in God and His joy is proof of that.

Encouragement Scripture

John 15:8

"When you produce much fruit, you are my true disciples. This brings great glory to my Father."

TRUTH LACED WITH GRACE

CHARIS ROOKS

Day 17

Affirmation

God's Power Is Strongest When I Am Weak

Devotion

God's power can be most strongly felt when we are at our weakest. He is there for us in times of ease, but He is especially present in times of trouble when we need help and when we need encouragement. He is there to help ease our fears, ease our troubles, and make our difficult times easier to bear and easier to deal with. Each time that there is trouble and each time we come to a road block on our path to our true purpose, He is waiting to lift us up over the hurdle and set us back on the path that He created for us.

Encouragement Scripture

2 Corinthians 12:9

"Each time He said, "My grace is all you need. My power works best in weakness." So now I am glad to boast about my weaknesses, so that the power of Christ can work through me."

TRUTH LACED WITH GRACE

CHARIS ROOKS

Day 18

Affirmation

My Faith Makes Me Whole

Devotion

There are times when you will feel incomplete and when you will feel that you are missing something, but know that your faith and your devotion make you whole. No matter how desolate you feel, how incomplete, the faith that you have in Jesus, in God, and in the Word, is enough to fill any space or lack that you might be feeling. Your faith makes you the whole, fantastic, and the powerful person that God designed you to be.

Encouragement Scripture

Mark 5:34

"And He said to her, "Daughter, your faith has made you well. Go in peace. Your suffering is over.""

TRUTH LACED WITH GRACE

CHARIS ROOKS

TRUTH LACED WITH GRACE

Affirmation

My Obedience to My Calling Keeps Me in Jesus' Love

Devotion

It might seem at times like straying from the path that has been chosen for you is the best way to go. The truth, however, is that your obedience to Jesus and to God is what helps keep you in grace of the Savior. Remaining obedient, even when times are difficult, even when you feel like there is nothing left, will let Jesus and God know that you are serious in your path. Jesus is there for you, and his love is guaranteed by your obedience and your mutual love for Him and for God.

Encouragement Scripture

John 15:10

"When you obey my commandments, you remain in my love, just as I obey my Father's commandments and remain in His love."

TRUTH LACED WITH GRACE

CHARIS ROOKS

Day 20

Affirmation

God Is My Strength He Will Always Help Me in Times of Need

Devotion

There are going to be times in your life when it seems like you have been abandoned by God. Though these times are few and far between, they serve a purpose.

These times when you start to lose faith serve to let you know that God is your strength, that He is always there, and that He will come to you in times of need. God works in ways that we are not attuned to. He works to make it seem the most desolate before He raises you up to reassure you that even in times of trouble, He is there to help ease your mind and set you on the path toward your ultimate purpose.

Encouragement Scripture

Psalm 46:1

"God is our refuge and strength, always ready to help in times of trouble."

TRUTH LACED WITH GRACE

CHARIS ROOKS

Affirmation

God Is More Powerful Than I Can Fathom; He Can Do More in My Life Than I Could Ever Imagine

Devotion

We work to achieve our goals. We set out boundaries, and we work to make sure that we have everything in our lives that we could ever want for. What many people fail to understand is that even when we work so hard, God can do more in our lives in one second than we can do with an entire life of toil and strife. The key is to give God the "go ahead" to do what He needs to do to raise us up and to make us into the person and the image that He wants for us. We can spend our entire lives working, but without giving God the ability and the freedom to work within us, we can never know what amazing things He has planned for us.

Encouragement Scripture

Ephesians 3:20

"Now all glory to God, who is able, through His mighty power at work within us, to accomplish infinitely more than we might ask or think."

TRUTH LACED WITH GRACE

CHARIS ROOKS

Day 22

Affirmation

I Will Live by Faith, Not by Sight, Even When Times Are Difficult

Devotion

It is all too easy for us to imagine that we are not enough and that things are going terribly wrong. We should work to live by faith rather than by sight. Live in the knowledge that even when things seem terrible, even when things seem like they are going wrong, there is a reason for it. God works to make sure that even when times are tough, even when it seems like things are going wrong, if you have faith, He will work to carry you through. God will help you get over any hurdle that has been set before you.

CHARIS ROOKS

Encouragement Scripture

2 Corinthians 5:7

For we live by faith, not by sight.

TRUTH LACED WITH GRACE

CHARIS ROOKS

Day 23

Affirmation

I Will Let God Ease My Troubles

Devotion

We often internalize things that we have no real control over. We work to take care of our own problems without ever reaching out for help of any kind. For those that follow the faith, God is there to ease your troubles. When you are down or when you are going through something that you simply cannot handle on your own, God is there to help raise you up and ease your troubles. We simply must let go, let God, and allow Him to handle the troubles that are weighing heavy on our hearts.

Encouragement Scripture

John 14:1

Jesus, the Way to the Father

"Don't let your hearts be troubled. Trust in God, and trust also in me."

TRUTH LACED WITH GRACE

CHARIS ROOKS

Day 24

Affirmation

God Sees the Good in My Heart

Devotion

We feel inadequate, we feel that we are not enough, and we feel that our outward actions do not reflect what we feel in our hearts far too often. God, however, sees what is in our hearts no matter what we do. We can act like we do not care, and we can act like we are okay on our own, but God can see what we have in our hearts. So, even if you stray from the path, even if you do something you should not have done, God can see your pure heart and He can work His ways within you to get you back on the path to right.

Encouragement Scripture

1 Samuel 16:7

"But the Lord said to Samuel, "Don't judge by his appearance or height, for I have rejected him. The Lord doesn't see things the way you see them. People judge by outward appearance, but the Lord looks at the heart."

TRUTH LACED WITH GRACE

CHARIS ROOKS

Day 25

Affirmation

God Is Always Guiding Me Towards My Purpose

Devotion

God always has His eye on the ultimate prize. Even when we stray or slip off the path, God always has His eyes on the goal that He has set for you. This is a great blessing for us as followers of Christ because, even when we start to lose sight of our end goal, He is always watching and can help redirect us to our purposes. Though you should work to keep the purpose in mind, you do not have to worry, because God will always help you find your way back.

Encouragement Scripture

1 John 4:4

"But you belong to God, my dear children. You have already won a victory over those people, because the Spirit who lives in you is greater than the spirit who lives in the world."

TRUTH LACED WITH GRACE

CHARIS ROOKS

Day 26

Affirmation

I Will Experience Life as Jesus Intended

Devotion

It might not always seem like things are going as planned, but a life with faith and a life with the love of Jesus and God is a life that is so worth living. A life with Jesus Christ is a life that is so full, so worthy, and so fantastic, and Jesus and God have set their plan into action to help you toward the goal that they have created for you. Life with Christ is a life that is lived as he intended, and your love of God and Christ will help see you through every time. God set your path before you were ever born, and you are on the right path. A life with Jesus is a life well lived.

Encouragement Scripture

1 John 5:12

"Whoever has the Son has life; whoever does not have God's Son does not have life."

TRUTH LACED WITH GRACE

CHARIS ROOKS

Day 27

Affirmation

God's Love Endures Forever

Devotion

There are times when we feel like we have lost favor with God and with Jesus. The truth is, however, that His love is forever. Once you give your life to Christ, you are always loved. You can sin, ask for forgiveness, and stray from the path repeatedly, but Jesus and God will never lose faith in you. They will never forsake you, and they will never lose the love that they have for you. Going about each day knowing that you are forever loved can make even the worst, the hardest, and the most troubling days seem like a walk in the park and that is the glory of God's love.

Encouragement Scripture

Jeremiah 33:11

"The sounds of joy and laughter. The joyful voices of bridegrooms and brides will be heard again, along with the joyous songs of people bringing thanksgiving offerings to the Lord. They will sing, 'Give thanks to the Lord of Heaven's armies, for the Lord is good. His faithful love endures forever!' For I will restore the prosperity of this land to what it was in the past, says the Lord."

TRUTH LACED WITH GRACE

CHARIS ROOKS

Day 28

Affirmation

Do Not Dwell on Your Mistakes.

Devotion

The most wonderful thing about our God is that He is a forgiving and loving God. You can make mistakes or bad decisions, and if you are sincere in your request for forgiveness, He will forgive you. This enduring love, this forever forgiveness, makes it so much easier to attain the life that He wants for you. Even if you sin, if you stop believing for a time, if you have trouble, God is always going to love you, and He will forgive any transgression that we commit. Life would be so much better if people were the same - if they could forgive and love one another, as God always does.

Encouragement Scripture

Hebrews 8:12

"And I will forgive their wickedness, and I will never again remember their sins."

TRUTH LACED WITH GRACE

CHARIS ROOKS

Day 29

Affirmation

If I Don't Believe in Something I Will Fall for Anything

Devotion

We have all heard the adage that if you do not believe in something, you will fall for anything. This is so true, especially when it comes to faith and God. Faith can only work its miracles when it is strong and has a very deeply rooted base. Faith that is faltering, faith that is fragile, and faith that is a front, is not going to deliver you into the graces of God and it is not going to guarantee that God is there for you. The stronger your faith and the greater your peace, the more that God will reach out to bless you and help you in your life. God cannot make you strong unless you believe in Him and allow Him to work through you.

Encouragement Scripture

Isaiah 7:9

"Israel is no stronger than its capital, Samaria, and Samaria is no stronger than its king, Pekah son of Remaliah. Unless your faith is firm, I cannot make you stand firm."

TRUTH LACED WITH GRACE

CHARIS ROOKS

Day 30

Affirmation

My Competence Comes from God, He Has My Purpose

Devotion

One of the biggest hang ups for most is that they do not feel that they are worthy, they do not feel qualified, and they do not feel competent. Our competence does not come from ourselves, but rather, from God. He makes us competent, He makes us worthy, and He makes us able to do all things through His love and through the love of Jesus Christ. The world is full of people that will continually work to break you down so that they can build themselves up. They are going to try to tell you that you are not worth it, that you are not strong enough, and that you are not ever going to amount to anything - and they are so wrong. God makes us worthy, and it is up to us to figure out what to do with that worthiness.

Encouragement Scripture

2 Corinthians 3:5

"It is not that we think we are qualified to do anything on our own. Our qualification comes from God."

TRUTH LACED WITH GRACE

CHARIS ROOKS

Day 31

Affirmation

I Will Not Abide by Negativity

Devotion

Negativity is something that makes us feel like we are not going to be able to do what we want in life. The secret is that negativity does not come from God - negativity comes from Satan. Since negativity is not something that is given to us by God, it is not something that we have to pay any attention to at all. We choose to let negativity eat away at us like a cancer, but God is the best medicine. Believe in yourself, push the negativity to the side, and allow God to do his greatest work within you each day no matter what you think.

Encouragement Scripture

2 Timothy 1:7

"For God has not given us a spirit of fear and timidity, but of power, love, and self-discipline."

TRUTH LACED WITH GRACE

CHARIS ROOKS

Additional Thoughts and Reflections

CHARIS ROOKS

TRUTH LACED WITH GRACE

CHARIS ROOKS

About the Author

CHARIS ROOKS

In a world that sometimes seems dead set to see people fail, Charis Rooks works to spread the word about Christ and his enduring love through her own personal testimony. Through her personal testimony, her dedication, and her love of God, Charis hopes to help the women that read her books to understand how truly special, truly wonderful, and truly powerful they are. The world needs more leaders, and now more than ever, it needs women that are God fearing and that are dedicated to Christ and to sharing their own personal testimony to build other women up rather than break them down.

When she is not working to empower her fellow women, Charis loves spending time with her husband, daughters, and grandson. She and her family currently live in Kentucky where she has completed her Bachelor's degree in Business Technical Management with a concentration in Small Business Management and Entrepreneurship. Charis completed her MBA in Leadership at Oral Roberts University and is now pursuing her Master of Divinity. Charis leads by example, and works to show women that though feelings of inadequacy can hurt a woman, it cannot break her.

Charis is passionate about speaking the truth and working to spread the word of Christ and its healing power. In addition to founding Divorce Recovery Advocates for Women INC., Charis is teacher of the word, speaker, Life after Divorce Care facilitator, and a facilitator for Divorce Care support groups. Charis currently serves as a Celebrate Recovery Training Coach at Harmony Christian Church, under the leadership of Dr. Billy Strother, member of the Professional Women's Network, member of the American Association of Christian Counselors and the International Christian Coaching Association, celebrated author, and Editor in Chief/CEO of Inspired Grace Media Productions.

Charis has also achieved several certifications including being certified as an International Women's Leadership Coach with a specialization in women's empowerment, confidence building, and professionalism. She has also achieved certification with the American Association of Christian Counselors as a life coach with a specialization in life after divorce coaching. Charis is the author of "Gods Rarest Diamonds: A Proverbs Life after Divorce Devotional for Women," "The 30-Day Life after Divorce Prayer Challenge for Women," and now, "Truth Laced with Grace."

Charis is dedicated to her craft and to making sure that every woman who is struggling knows that there is hope, there is a way to succeed. Charis is a dedicated individual who wants nothing more than to share her ideas, experiences, and knowledge to help other women who are struggling to become comfortable with themselves, with the state of their lives again, as well as help them to achieve the calling that God has created for them. Through Christ, anything is possible, and with the right tools, anyone can succeed no matter how difficult the task is set before them. Through Christ, so many wonderful things are possible, and Charis hopes to lead by example and show women everywhere that they are capable of so much more than they ever thought possible.

Contact Information

Divorce Recovery Advocates for Women INC Website: www.draw4women.com Email: info@draw4women.com

Facebook: https://www.facebook.com/draw4women and http://www.facebook.com/charismrooksoutreachministries

Twitter: Charis Rooks@draw4women

Instagram: Draw4Women

Inspired Grace Media Productions LLC
http://www.igmproductions.com

Facebook
https://www.facebook.com/InspiredGraceMediaProduction

www.ingramcontent.com/pod-product-compliance
Lightning Source LLC
Chambersburg PA
CBHW070159100426
42743CB00013B/2969